The "n"-Word...

Explained!!!

The "n"-Word...

Explained!!!

"For the Socially Progressive"

By: <u>Charles E. Dickerson</u>

Neo Nexus Publishing, LLC

COLUMBIA, SOUTH CAROLINA

*

ISBN-10: 0-9846673-5-0
ISBN-13: 978-0-98466735-2
Library of Congress Control Number: 2015903492

*

Copyright © Charles E. Dickerson 2 0 1 8
Second Edition
ALL RIGHTS RESERVED.
No part of this publication is to be reproduced in any manner without prior written permission from the publisher.

*

PRINTED IN THE UNITED STATES OF AMERICA.

Reference Sources:

Encyclopedia Britannica

Wikipedia Encyclopedia

Merriam-Webster Dictionary

United States Census Bureau

Online Etymology Dictionary

Ava DuVernay
Documentary "13th"

NAACP
Criminal Justice Fact Sheet

Teachers.net Gazette
December 2005, Vol 2, No 12

United States Constitution
13th Amendment, Sections 1 & 2

Library of Congress
Prints & Photos, Online Catalog

The Los Angeles Times
November 14, 2012 - By Danielle Ryan

WWW-Virtual Library: History
*Map History / History of Cartography:
The Gateway to the Subject*

Ferris State University (FSU)
Jim Crow Museum of Racist Memorabilia

Emory University - Voyages Database
The Trans-Atlantic Slave Trade

Thirteen/WNET New York
Educational Broadcasting Corporation
"Slavery and the Making of America"

Dr. Yosef Ben Jochannan
Black Man of the Nile and his Family

Dr. Henry Louis Gates, Jr.
The African Americans: Many Rivers To Cross

Courtesy of The African American Registry
Dr. David Pilgrim and Phil Middleton
"Nigger (The Word), A Brief History"

Dr. Neil A. Frankel
The Atlantic Slave Trade And Slavery In America

Gomes Eanes de Azurara
Chronicle of the Discovery and Conquest of Guinea (1896)

Lerone Bennett, Jr.
Before The Mayflower: A History of Black America 1619-1964

AlterNet: Adam Hudson
"1 Black Man Is Killed Every 28 Hours by Police or Vigilantes: America Is Perpetually at War with Its Own People"

Contents

Dedication	viii
Foreword	ix
Trans-Atlantic Slave Trade	1
Slavery, Property and *"nigger"*... Ethnicity erased	11
The "n"-Word Explained	24
Nigger... A *"Generic* or *Trade Label" "racial epitaph"*	26
Word *"nigger"* survives all wars and rebellions	26
Word *"nigger"* memorialized and buried, yet it lives	27
The new teachers of cultural disenlightenment	29
Cultural & social implications of the word nigger	29
The Word *"nigger"* revisited at its source	33
African slavery and its people	34
The *"Middle Passage"* and its *"floating hell holes"*	36
A once glorious people lost in cultural translation	37
West Africans... Targets of European possession	39
Niger region... Targeted areas of slave acquisition	41
How the word *"nigger"* came to be	43
Trans-Atlantic Slave Trade and its vestiges	44
Origin and evolution of the word *"nigger"*	47
Nigger... An *"Interim Identifier"* or *"Racial Slur"*	50
Nigger... From private property to state property	51
Prison behavior supplants early Hip Hop culture	52
Loss of public sentiment... Key to social injustice	53
The Casual Killing Act	56
Casual Killing Act once dead... Now resurrected	57

Contents

Self-castigation an enemy unto itself	58
Importance of sticking to who we are as a people	58
America and her double standard toward Blacks	60
Positive image presentation fuels public sentiment	61
Negative image presentation comes with a cost	62
Becoming a Personal Property Candidate is a choice	63
We desperately need to clean up our act	64
Black freedom… A different kind of freedom	64
A new generation in stark contrast to the old	65
Freedom & public sentiment… old social currencies	66
America's ongoing war with her own people	67
President Obama's election prompts secession call	69
Property and *"nigger"*… Inextricably linked	70
Publisher's Note	72
Cultural Acknowledgment	73

Dedicated to...

~~~

The socially progressive individuals living in modern cultures and civilized societies throughout the western world.

The *"presence"* and *"power"* in a name is important. If not, man's first assignment from God would not have been to assign names to all of the animals.

As people, we have a duty and obligation to demonstrate common courtesy and mutual respect toward one another.

If everyone were addressed by "Name", instead of being called *"other things"*, the world would be a better place.

Our names and titles are unique to our *"character"* and *"person"*, we are to honor, respect, and use them.

~~~

~ *Foreword* ~

This is a story of Africa's modern day descendants, whom were forcefully domiciled in the Americas as slaves. The story began as an unbelievable tale of nightmarish proportion that would ultimately redefine the *treatment boundaries* and *subject identity* of captives taken into slavery.

In times past, prior to the Trans-Atlantic Slave Trade, slavery was based solely upon the loss of one's freedom, wherein the enslaved person or individuals became the servant property of another. In fact, slavery is not new; slavery has existed in various nations and lands since the dawn of mankind.

> Merriam-Webster Dictionary defines slavery as...
> *"the state of a person who is a chattel of another"*,
> in addition to defining chattel as... *"something (such as a slave, piece of furniture, tool, etc.) that a person owns other than land or buildings."*

African slavery existed long before there was an America and did not have its beginning with the Trans-Atlantic Slave Trade. Slavery in the Americas sprang from the birth of European enslavement of Africans that had its beginning in the year 1441 A.D. with the Portuguese, whom initiated the practice of forcefully capturing and kidnapping Africans for the purpose of trading them to other Europeans.

American slavery was considerably different from earlier forms of slavery dating back to the ancient civilizations of the Samaritans, Egyptians, Byzantines and the Ottomans, among others. The earliest official record of slavery can be traced back to 1760 B.C. in Samaria, wherein the following is recorded in the <u>Code of Hammurabi</u>: {Example: Law #15}

"If any one take a male or female slave of the court, or a male or female slave of a freed man, outside the city gates, he shall be put to death."

Those who lost their freedom to slavery prior to the Trans-Atlantic Slave Trade were fortunate considering they were allowed to retain their *cultural identities*. Unlike British colonial slavery in America, wherein the slaves were stripped of their <u>generational, historical, social, religious, ethnic,</u> and <u>personal identities</u>, which in effect constitutes <u>*"institutionally, prescribed nigger-dom"*. In fact, identity theft is believed to be a recent phenomenon, but it had its beginning with African slaves!!!</u>

For this cause, Black People have a vested interest in learning the true knowledge of their cultural past that existed long before British colonial slavery. The ancestral knowledge of Blacks is essential to erasing the awful stigma that has been ascribed to us by the slave merchants and slave masters of yesterday.

Shipping logs provided by <u>*Voyages: The Trans-Atlantic Slave Trade Database*</u> show 12,521,336 captives were transported into the Americas (1501 – 1866), including 305,326 that entered into North America (1619 – 1865). For 246 years African slaves were treated as *"sub-humans"* and trade-labelled *"niggers"*. <u>Dreadfully, the tens of millions that were kidnapped, smuggled, pirated and perished have gone undocumented!!!</u>

♛	Spain / Uruguay	Portugal / Brazil	Great Britain	Netherlands	U.S.A.	France	Denmark / Baltic	Totals
1501-1600	119,962	154,191	1,922	1,365	0	66	0	277,506
1601-1700	146,270	1,011,192	428,262	219,931	4,151	38,435	27,391	1,875,631
1701-1800	10,654	2,213,003	2,545,297	330,014	189,304	1,139,013	67,334	6,494,619
1801-1866	784,639	2,469,879	283,959	3,026	111,871	203,890	16,316	3,873,580
Totals	1,061,524	5,848,265	3,259,440	554,336	305,326	1,381,404	111,041	12,521,336

In the aftermath of the American Civil War the

emancipated slaves were treated as *"last-class citizens"* after being declared free. Unfortunately, the *"last-class designation"* that was previously assigned to the slaves during slavery *(without citizenship)* was now coupled with lingering *"racially social dynamics"* among the White populous that engendered the continued use of the word *"nigger"*. Even casual use of the word negatively affects many Blacks, causing a distorted view of one's personal and collective identity.

*I*n 1865 the legal status of *"nigger"* was <u>annulled</u> on the basis of *"property ownership"* and recast as *"Negro"*. This landmark decision would usher in an era of *"second-class citizenship"* without the affordability or guarantee of *"Equal Protection" or "Equal Opportunity"* under the Law, which would go unchecked for the next 100 years.

*Y*ou are invited to explore this extremely powerful and long over-due volume of work that serves as a precursor to its companion publication, *"From Kingdom to nigger-dom... A People Lost In Translation"*.

"From Kingdom to nigger-dom... A People Lost In Translation" goes into extraordinary detail on Black life as it were in times past, when *"slave", "property",* and *"nigger"* were primary identifiers for our ancestors, whom were subjected to the <u>overall slavery and Black experience</u> leading up to the present day.

According to the Merriam-Webster Dictionary...

> *"Nigger is an infamous word in current English, so much so that when people are called upon to discuss it, they more often than not refer to it euphemistically as "the N-word." Its offensiveness is not new – dictionaries have been noting it for more than 150 years – but it has grown more pronounced with the passage of time. The word now ranks as almost certainly the most offensive and inflammatory racial slur in English, a term expressive of hatred and bigotry."*

"The "n"-Word Explained" exposes the *origin, background, and social implications* of the continued usage of the so-called *"n"-Word* in the lives of Black People in America and other parts of the world. This unique body of work provides a patented introduction and detailed analysis into our gross misunderstanding and twisted interpretation into the *origin, history, and prolonged life cycle* of the outdated and much maligned use of the word *"nigger"*.

> *Did the word "nigger" have its beginning as a...*
> *"Generic Trade Label" or "Racial Slur"???*

This work has been written for everyone who is familiar with the 14th letter *("n")* of the English alphabet, realizing that not everyone that read this book will readily receive the message and agree with its content.

The *"unsavory truth"* is that any unwelcomed pattern of social behavior will not be completely extinguished until the teachers of such behavior die out. When the *"enlightened ones"* among us abandon its use, in due time the *"socially unacceptable use"* of the word *"nigger"* will eventually go away, thereby sanctioning its *"official death"* and *"proper burial"*.

The *"teachers"* in this particular case includes both White People and Black People alike, who profane the letter *"n"* by continuing to use the word *"nigger"* and its *"derivatives"*, which has been reintroduced into American society and it's lexicon as the *"n"-Word*.

This powerful and unique body of work exposes the need for a *paradigm shift* in the *racial attitudes*, and *social behaviors* of White Americans and Black Americans alike in North American society.

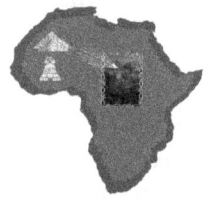

The purpose and intent of this publication is to serve as a clarion call to people of conscience, with the expressed desire of improving race relations between Black Americans and White Americans, who are plagued by the misgivings of the past, due to no fault of our own.

Refresh, relax, and enjoy the read!!!

Charles E. Dickerson

~ Trans-Atlantic Slave Trade ~

Africa's… Achilles' Heel!!!

History provides written record of a large number of Africans being kidnapped by the Portuguese in 1441 A.D. and taken to Portugal as slaves. This maiden event marked the beginning of what would ultimately become the Trans-Atlantic Slave Trade and the forged inception of the Black race into the Americas.

In 1441 A.D. Prince Henry *(3rd son of Portugal's King John 1)* initiated the first major European slaving expedition by sending six ships to West Africa under the command of Lançarote de Freitas, the Revenue Officer of Lagos. All of the ships were fitted with banners that read *"Order of Christ"*. The journey is recorded in *"The Chronicles of the Discovery and Conquest of Guinea"*, by its author Gomes Eanes de Azurara. Gomes Eanes de Azurara describes the Portuguese capture of 235 Africans that took place in the present day West African land of Mauritania.

> *"We saw the Moors with their women and children coming out of their huts as fast as they could, when they caught sight of their enemy. Our men, crying out St James, St George and Portugal, fell upon them killing and taking all they could.*
>
> *There you might have seen mothers catch up with their children, husbands, their wives, each one trying to flee as best he could. Some plunged into the sea, others thought to hide themselves in the corners of their hovels, others hid their children underneath the shrubs that grew about there, where our men found them."* *"And the Moors of that capture were in number 235."* {The Chronicles of the Discovery and Conquest

According to Azurara, the Portuguese raiders attacked several other villages returning with no less than 235 captives. All were taken to Lagos, Portugal where on August 8, 1444 they were marched to a meadow on the outskirts of town where the first European slave auction was held. Reportedly, Gomes Eanes de Azurara was there and was terribly moved by the treatment of the Guinea captives.

In the year 1445 A.D. Prince Henry established the first European slave market and fort in Arguin Bay, Lagos for the purpose of auctioning the kidnapped Africans into slavery that had been forcefully acquired beginning four years earlier. It is here that the Atlantic Slave Trade began. Prince Henry's introduction of *"Portuguese slave raiding"* would later morph into *"systematically coerced trans-Atlantic slave trading"* throughout the North American hemisphere.

Just a couple of centuries later on Bunce Island in Sierra Leone and other parts of western Africa,

Africans were trading Africans to Europeans in the thousands for guns, liquor, money, fine apparel and other commodities. According to Dr. Henry Louis Gates, Jr. over half of the African captives that were forced into slavery were sold by Africans during the course of the Trans-Atlantic Slave Trade.

The Trans-Atlantic Slave Trade was a *"European initiated commercial enterprise"* that was foundered upon the supremacy of power, merciless and ruthless attacks, domination, violence and coercion, only for it to evolve into a mutual partnership with the less militarized West Africans that lasted until the end of the American Civil War. What began as a Portuguese inspired, coerced business venture would later escalate into all-out human poaching, village raids and systematic kidnappings by European and African headhunters, who began to view all West Africans as a human source of potential wealth. It is important to note that tribal wars resulting in the selling of the captured from defeated tribes fueled the birth of homegrown slavery in Africa long before the Trans-Atlantic Slave Trade began.

Africans of all ages, genders, trades and vocations were captured, marched, dragged and hauled aboard the awaiting slave ships that docked in the various ports of entry to load their human cargo. Fleets of ships were draped with *"banners of Christ"*, including one in particular that was named after Jesus. These ships were later crammed and stuffed beyond capacity with African captives from all walks of life before embarking upon the 8 to 10 months voyages that crisscrossed the Atlantic Ocean to reach *"Europe"* and the *"New World"*.

"16th Century Slave Cargo Ship"

"Jesus of Lübeck"

"Jesus of Lübeck became involved in the Trans-Atlantic slave trade under John Hawkins, who organized four voyages to West Africa and the West Indies between 1562 and 1568.

During the last voyage, Jesus, along with several other English ships, encountered a Spanish fleet off <u>San Juan de Ulúa</u> (modern day

Vera Cruz, Mexico) in September 1568.

In the <u>resulting battle</u>, Jesus was captured by Spanish forces. The heavily damaged ship was later sold for 601 <u>ducats</u> to a local merchant." {Wikipedia Encyclopedia}

Africans of all backgrounds and classifications were <u>hunted, herded, stolen, branded and traded</u> by professed Christians of European religious persuasion before being sold individually and in mixed groups *(small and large)* to the European and American slave merchants, whom auctioned them off to the *"rich and soon to be wealthy landowners"* in Europe and the barren lands and islands in the Americas.

Data retrieved from the shipping logs of <u>*Voyages: The Trans-Atlantic Slave Trade Database*</u> provides records of 12,521,336 captives being transported into the Americas *(1501 A.D. – 1866 A.D.)*, including 305,326 that entered into North America *(1619 A.D. – 1865 A.D.)*. For 246 years African slaves were treated as *"sub-humans"* and trade-labelled *"niggers"*. <u>Dreadfully, tens of millions more were kidnapped, smuggled, and pirated, whom perished and have gone undocumented!!!</u>

It is here among the millions of Africans issuing out of *lost religions, customs, tongues and tribes* that the trans-Atlantic slavery story took root and flourished in the mining camps, sugarcane groves, tobacco lands and plantations in the West Indies, Europe, North America, South America and Central America.

The dreaded Africans boarded the slave ships as deposed village kings, queens, tribal chiefs, priests, doctors, artists, artisans, musicians, farmers, spinners, weavers, herdsmen, tradesmen, among various other craftsmen and laborers, only to be cast to the bottom of the social, economic and human rungs of European, American and Caribbean societies, where a large number of Blacks find themselves today.

This is a book of cultural ambivalence that has been written and compiled for the ones of us that have been lost in cultural translation, seeking an explanation to how our own people could have sold us into slavery. It also begs an answer to how the Europeans that <u>kidnapped, stole</u> and <u>forced-purchased us</u> could have subjected us to an *"unprecedented institutional system of abuse"* and *"nigger-dom"* that erased our ethnicity with the intent of paralyzing our human growth and quarantining us in a state of cultural ignorance that would forever bind us to a system of free labor.

Unfortunately, our loss of ethnicity rendered us equivalent to a *"bouquet of roses"* in comparison to the Europeans and Asians that migrated to North America with their cultural roots intact. The flourishing of their native ethnicity and culture is evident in the American economy emanating from the cultural ingredients and recipes of their native ethnicity. We on the other hand were stripped of our cultural identity upon being forged into a foreign land and profoundly racist culture without the freedom and cultural tools to properly translate and assimilate as migrant citizens. The slaves were transfixed in a distorted space and skewed time, due to the severing of their cultural roots of ethnicity. The results engendered the most horrific form of slavery inflicted upon a people in the entire history of man.

To better understand the *"prescribed damage"* that was done due to the lack of knowledge concerning our *"native culture"*, we need only compare a *"rosebush"* that is planted in the ground to a *"bouquet of roses"* that is deposited in a vase <u>without a root</u>. Upon comparing the two it is apparent that a rosebush that is rooted will outlive the planter. Unlike a bouquet of roses that cannot survive without a root, thus causing it to wither and die. The rosebush being rooted allows it to draw the essential life sustaining nutrients from its native soil, versus a bouquet that is artificially confined in a container that is similar in function to a *"plantation"*, thus depriving it of the vital nutrients that are necessary for it to adapt, flourish and grow.

Without root the bouquet blooms but never blossoms, whereby each individual stem is forced to rely solely upon itself, thus guaranteeing a futile existence. The bouquet survives for a very brief period as a group of individual stems, but never survives as a collective unit to bloom, blossom and reproduce generationally over and over and over again, perpetually. The stems of the bouquet strives separated, being individually supported by the vase <u>because there is no root</u> to nourish, strengthen and support the stems collectively, thus rendering the bouquet the most vulnerable of any plant on Earth. The bouquet lives for a short period of time being separated into individual parts of a whole before it withers and dies for lack of nourishment, requiring constant care prior to being replaced in a newly recurring cycle that begins again and again at zero.

Worst of all... the bouquet has to start over from scratch after each and every passing generation and when placed alongside the *"ethnic rose bushes of the world"* that are rooted, unified, resilient and vibrantly strong the bouquet is not ably equipped to collectively compete nor stand. <u>The bouquet is incapable of regrowing its root due to lack of life, but with dedication to the study of our history we are indeed able!!!</u>

Fortunately, slavery was abolished on April 9, 1865 in North America when the Confederate Army was defeated by the Union Army, rendering its government, monetary currency and slave-based economy nonexistent. Yet many slaves did not learn of their freedom until months later, on June 19, 1865; this date is traditionally observed by Black Americans as the *"Juneteenth Celebration"*. Unfortunately, the property aspect of slavery transformed the once free Africans into a *"slave commodity"*, wherein the word *"nigger"* would become a *"property brand"* equivalent in magnitude to that of *Google, Apple, Microsoft, Nike, Facebook, Pepsi and Coca Cola,* which is yet to be erased.

Ironically, even though the Africans and their American born descendants were no longer *"legal property"*, the *"property brand"* was permanently affixed to them and continues to be used today as a degrading and *"derogatory racial brand"*, even though the *"chattel property"* status no longer <u>legally exist</u>. Yet Whites continue to engage the so-called *"n"-Word* to denote *"derogatory branding"* and Blacks embrace it as an *"endearing cultural marker"*, wherein both are ignorant of the fact that it was a *"<u>commercial property brand</u>"* denoting a *"geographical place of origin"* in the West African interior of *"Niger"*, where innocent fathers, mothers, sisters, brothers and little children were forcefully extracted, traded and sold for profit.

The use of the word *"nigger"* by Whites and Blacks represents the continuing vulgar indulgence of the mutually agreed upon arrangement by the early Europeans and Africans who stole, bought and sold <u>*innocent people*</u> into slavery when the Trans-Atlantic Slave Trade began. <u>***This is an irony and a travesty!!!***</u>

Slavery, Property and Nigger!!!
Ethnicity… Erased!!!

"But many that are first shall be last, and the last shall be first."

A prophetic verse from the first…
Foreshadowing Africa's slavery birth!
~ Matthew 19:30 ~

Since the earliest of times slavery has existed in one form or another, wherein one individual or group have subjected others to forced servitude for the purpose of extracting free labor. The primary motivation for slavery is to rid oneself of the toils of labor by forcing the hideous responsibility upon another without residual cost.

The *Trans-Atlantic Slave Trade* was uniquely different from earlier forms of slavery, in that it robbed its subjects of their ethnic identities. For 444 years the less militarized, less organized, disenfranchised West Africans were exploited by generations of rich and powerful European colonists and corporate investors for the purpose of personal gain and perpetual profit.

More than twenty two generations of West African citizens whom were gainful, intelligent, productive, law abiding individuals were reduced to the level of *"private possession in the form of chattel property"* and brought to America as *"native savages"* and counted as *"three-fifths of a man"* in the United States Constitution.

The Trans-Atlantic Slave Trade was West African natives of the land of **Nigrita**, being bought and stole, caught and sold, before being traded by their frightened old village chief for apparel and a few bottles of brandy and rum, only for the guilt-ridden chief to be kidnapped and sold into slavery several weeks, months, or years later.

The Trans-Atlantic Slave Trade was being born with a slave bounty on your head, because your pregnant African mother gave birth while passing through the land of **Nigro**.

The Trans-Atlantic Slave Trade was going for a Sunday walk in the land of **Nigriti**, and months later being sold to the highest bidder at the Old Slave Mart in Charleston, South Carolina. In the mid-1850s slave prices ranged from $100.00 upward to $1450.00 depending upon age, sex, family grouping, physical condition, special skills, and other appraisal criteria.

The Trans-Atlantic Slave Trade was going hunting in the forest of **Negro Land**, only to be stalked, poached, trapped, and branded with an "x" on your chest before being sold to an awaiting ship captain headed for the Caribbean.

The Trans-Atlantic Slave Trade was being kidnapped from the land of **Nigritie**, before being beaten, branded, and sold into Christian slavery, while receiving the enslaving captain's wholesale blessing of baptism in the name of God the Father, God the Son, and God the Holy Spirit.

The Trans-Atlantic Slave Trade was being captured from the land of **Nigritia**, and later auctioned into slavery to work in the rice fields of South Carolina, where according to Dr. Henry Louis Gates Jr. 1/3 of the slaves died from snake bite, and malaria in the first year, and 2/3 of the children were dead before they reached their 16th birthday.

The Trans-Atlantic Slave Trade was the inability to run

faster than a gazelle, and camouflage yourself better than a leopard, resulting in your ending up in a cage headed for the port of Sierra Leone for shipment to Brazil.

The Trans-Atlantic Slave Trade was husbands, wives, mothers, and babies crying, brothers, sisters, and children dying of self-inflicted wounds rather than becoming slaves.

The Trans-Atlantic Slave Trade was having gashes, cuts, and bruises on your back, an iron mask on your face, and an iron collar around your neck, because you were discovered to be an African tribal warrior upon being captured.

The Trans-Atlantic Slave Trade was being a Black African king, queen, doctor, translator, or priest, only to pass through "The Door Of No Return" in Senegal West Africa with chains on your arms, and shackles on your legs, while in route to the gold mines, sugar, rice, cotton, coffee, and tobacco fields of the Americas to work without pay forever, and never see your family, and homeland again.

These examples are just a mere fraction of the

countless atrocities that took place beginning with and during the Trans-Atlantic Slave Trade, when America's Blacks were forged into existence as a **"<u>separate and distinct race of people, whose heritage and ethnicity was erased</u>"**. The slaves experienced a *"genetic transformation"* stemming from the unwelcomed, and unavoidable sexual encounters and abuses that occurred between the slaves' powerful and controlling European slave masters, and our helpless African and African American ancestors.

This predominate factor accounts for the wide ranging differences in skin complexions, phenotypes, and hues among Blacks that further skew and fracture our collective and individual sense of ethnic identity. The *"<u>obvious lack of ethnic unity</u>"* among Black's is basically nonexistent in other ethnic groups that operate on the basis of "COLONY" in America.

Far too many Blacks embrace the notion that colonization has passed, when in fact all ethnic groups in America operate on the basis of *"self-imposed colony"* except us; colloquially speaking, the saying... **"<u>Blacks don't stick together</u>"** is true. Unfortunately, the foundational pillars of *"colony"*, which are *"<u>ethnic unity</u>"*, *"<u>economic independence</u>"* and *"<u>political power</u>"* that were forged into existence by Jim Crow were alive and well in the Black community prior to July 2, 1964, only to be abandoned gradually for *"<u>ACCESS</u>"* leading to *"integration"* in the overall quest for *"Civil Rights"*.

In America there exist two colony groups, a *"Greater Colony Group"* and a *"Lesser Colony Group"*. The *"Greater Colony Group"* is composed of the various Caucasian ethnic groups that collectively make up the power structure in America. The *"Lesser Colony Group"* is composed of the minority ethnic groups that have migrated here from around the world that band together to ensure their *"ethnic unity"*, *"economic independence"* and *"political power"* for the sake of common good. Unfortunately, we do not fit into either group from a collective standpoint.

Each of the *"lesser colonies"*, be they Native American, Mexican, Jewish, East Indian, Arab, Korean, Chinese, Vietnamese, Japanese, etc., abide by a *"Self-Imposed Colonial Code"* that endows them with the *"ethnic unity"*, *"economic independence"* and *"political power"* needed to move to the *"next level"*.

In this instance we are the exception; *we lack the "cultural knowledge of self" that unifies and strengthens us, to make us independent collectively, and interdependent upon one another*. Unfortunately, we do not function as a colony, and for this reason we exhaust the capital resources needed to capitalize on what we are able to do <u>collectively</u>. Our African and African American ancestors were extremely *able* and the *"building of America"* is standing proof.

Unlike the slave masters, they were capable (*"capable"*), simply because they had the much needed <u>capital</u> to resource the things that our ancestors were able to do... *"for them"*. Where on the other hand, we a bonded and unpaid people were not afforded the freedom or the resources to do the same for *"ourselves"*. In fact, *money, knowledge, and freedom* were treated like contraband requiring severe punishment.

To understand the importance of what I am saying, we need only review our generational group progress relative to the other ethnic groups in America going back 150 years to our freedom and after weighing the collective results, ask the question... <u>WHY?</u>

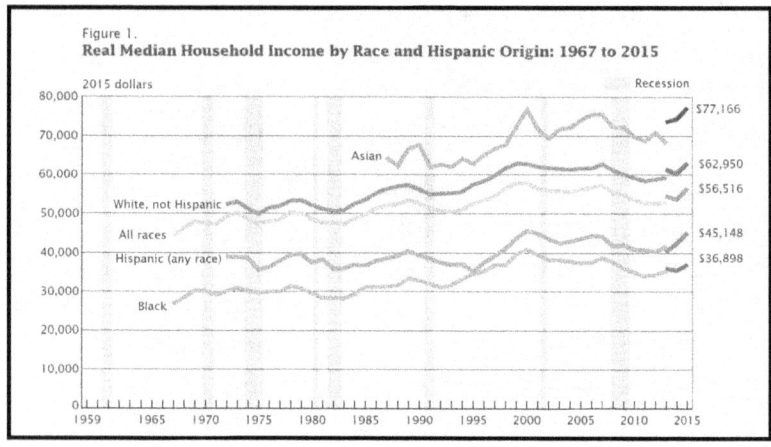

So why do all of the other ethnic groups in America show more positive and progressive signs of ethnic prosperity from generation to generation except us? Why is it that today we can go out and purchase a *British, Japanese, Chinese, German, Italian, French, Swedish, Korean* automobile, but not an *African or African American* automobile? Why is it that today we can go out and order *French, Italian, Mexican, Chinese, Japanese, Greek, German,* and many other types of ethnic foods, but in the majority of cities we cannot order *African* Food? <u>I would like to know why?</u>

Why is it that today we can go out and easily buy Italian suits and shoes, French perfumes, and the finest Yugoslavian led crystal, but it is hard if at all possible to find an African or African American button to sew onto the French suit, or an African or African American tire to mount onto the German car, or buy an African or African American sock to wear inside the Italian shoe, or purchase an African or African American spoon to eat the Greek food out of the Yugoslavian plate. *I would like to know why?*

This reminds me of something I heard many years ago spoken by an older African American minister...

> *"When things aren't going right, we don't need to be told by anyone that there's a dead cat on the line; you just know."*

So when we look around America today and see all of the other ethnic groups moving ahead generationally, while we are being left behind, we shouldn't need to be told that something is wrong, we should automatically know that something is wrong. And the question is... Is there something wrong in America, *or is there something wrong with us?*

When it comes to African Americans, there is no doubt that something is wrong in America, but the *"wrong in America"* will not change until we change the things that are wrong with us. So the first thing we need to do is to educate ourselves to understand what is meant by... *"moving to the next level"*. We have to rid ourselves of the notion that moving to the next level is an individual process based upon consumption. We have to understand that moving to the next level is not the act of buying a new or newer automobile, purchasing a bigger house, or getting a better job to consume more.

Moving to the next level is a collective process of transitioning from *"able"* to *"capable"* (*cap*-able) and this is done by learning what we can pour out of ourselves, rather than what we can take in through the process of indebtedness and consumption. More often than not we fall into the trap of buying into the *"low self-esteem scenario"* by rendering a low appraisal of ourselves based upon the adversary, without realizing that the root-word to self-esteem is *"teem"*, which is defined as... the process of *"pouring out"*.

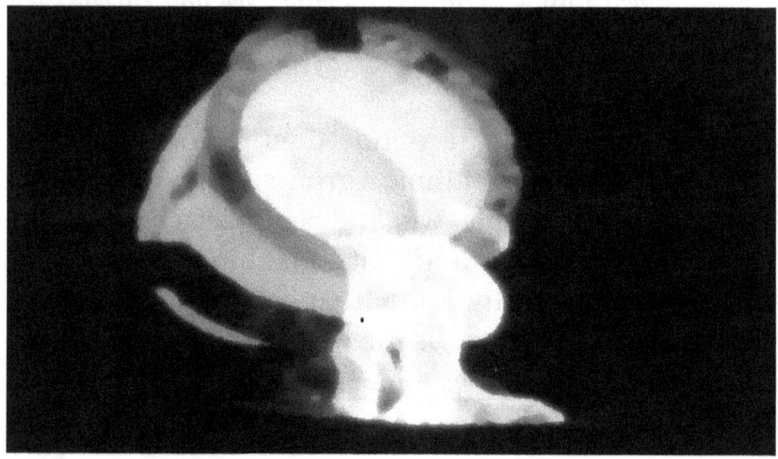

The word *"esteem"* comes from the process of appraisal, based upon estimated outpouring *(es-teem)*. Therefore, it is impossible to estimate what we can pour out of ourselves until we know and understand that which has been poured into us by our ancestors, and those that have come before us.

The appraised value of all things is based upon present condition, relative to the current and historic value of same or like pieces. In short, present and future value is based upon historical value. We the 21st century African Americans are placed in positions on a daily basis wherein we need an appraisal of ourselves to receive fair and equitable treatment and compensation. In these instances we must look deep within ourselves going back to our ancient ancestry of antiquity if needed, in order to determine our individual and collective worth.

*W*e cannot afford to allow others to continue to devaluate our *history, abilities, efforts, and contributions* on a daily basis, while chaperoning their histories and performance results to the forefront of life. When allowed, they dictate when and how we are to live and celebrate our *"Journey of Relationship"* with one another. When we allow others to dictate when and how we are to interpret and receive *"our Story"* they take away the good for themselves, leaving us with a *"bad report"*, *"bad position"*, and a *"bad name"*!

*W*e need to reconnect with our *"Total Experience"*, which is our *"collective truth"*, with the understanding that the largest and best part of our story has been *systematically distorted, plagiarized, and erased.* We have a current day example of this with the ongoing and recent effort of overturning the *"Affordable Care Act" and other legislation by President Obama*. This is a continuation of the 8 year mission undertaken by the racist conservative base in the Republican Party to dismantle and erase President Obama's historical legacy, which began on his very first day in office.

*O*ur daily job and individual responsibilities is to take back the legacy of our forefathers that have been stolen by allowing them to come alive again in us and dutifully pass them on to our young. We need to begin to view our history and hereditary story as a friend and not an adversary. We have been conditioned to celebrate the worst part of our history, while lacking the realization that our *"Total Experience"* reconnects us to the root of our heritage and our past. We can no longer afford to allow the psychological trappings of the Trans-Atlantic Slave Trade to determine our path and destines.

This and more is true, much to the chagrin of Black People who look at things as they are, with little concern or fore-thought being applied to how things use to be. There are many who would rather shut their eyes to the damaging effects of British colonial slavery by imagining the horrors and carnage of the Trans-Atlantic Slave Trade never happened.

We seriously need to examine ourselves in light of our fears and denial and then reach out to our youth in the *"spirit of truth, awareness, and understanding"* to make the "Black Experience" better for future generations.

"From Kingdom to nigger-dom" utilizes commentary, poetry, prose, and candid introspection of the Black historical journey to remind us of how things were in times past and in some instances still are. I believe poetry to be the *"unbridled voice"* and *"imaginative key"* of the changing times, which pierces the hearts, and stirs the minds of each and every passing generation.

This publication serves to remind us of a commonly overlooked fact when it comes to living the *"Black Experience"*. So let us not forget that Black life with all of its challenges, nuances, and intricacies has for itself the results of the experiential distance traveled, which often times is interpreted and expressed differently by those who have reached their destinations.

Some may view the distance traveled as a *"marvelous journey"*, wherein others might well view the distance traveled as only a *"trip"*. I believe Black life to be a *"collective journey defined by shared experiences"*, wherein the *"trip is defined by the destination sought"*, and oftentimes the experiential distance is traveled alone.

You are personally invited to journey through the cultural twists, turns, and nuances of the *"Collective Black Experience"* that is expressed in this most informative and provocative publication.

"From Kingdom to nigger-dom" provides a patented and historically candid introduction into the *"composite life experiences"* of *"Black People in North America"*. Ones who were racially branded and trade labelled *"niggers"* by white southerners residing in the British-American colonies. <u>You are encouraged to accept the experiential challenge of sharing the cultural journey!!!</u>

Buckle up, relax and enjoy the read!!!

Charles E. Dickerson

~ The "n"-Word Explained ~

Continuation of a misguided saga!!!

There are many who ask... *"Why have a discussion about the "n"-Word"?* Undoubtedly there is a lot of ambivalence and twisted emotions associated with the word *"nigger"* and rightfully so. Yet, a large number of people continue to breathe life into it even until this day. While others attempt to close their ears, while hoping that it will be buried alive or simply go away.

> **NAACP delegates 'bury' N-word in ceremony**
> 'We're taking it out of our spirit,' Detroit mayor says of racial slur

Yet, upon considering the magnitude of the social implications surrounding this extremely toxic and most incendiary word, I feel duty bound as a Black person, whom at the age of eight was subjected to and witnessed my mother being offended by its use, when I was called *"nigger"* by two middle aged adult Caucasian females, simply because I was Black.

This traumatic experience combined with the *"brewing controversy"* surrounding the continual use of the word provided the impetus needed to exhume and examine the *"alleged corpse"* at its source, which is absolutely essential to understanding its *origin, nature and prolonged life-cycle.* Unraveling the anguish, bitterness and pain that explains the social implications of the continued use of the word for nearly 400 years in the aftermath of its *"illegitimate birth"* has become a priority and a personal quest.

The *"n"-Word* as we have come to know it, has taken upon itself a stubborn resistance to social intolerance. The word has begun to live and thrive outside of the initial boundaries and social context in which it was initially prescribed.

Nigger... A Generic Trade Label or racial epitaph!!!

From its source, the word *"Niger"* served as a *"generic trade label"* springing forth from the <u>Niger region of West Africa</u> prior to derogatorily morphing into the word *"nigger"*. Wherein this simple little word matured and spread like a *"pandemic social disease"* that has continued to grow and function like a *"cancer"* without a cure.

Like all things that have life, the life that is perpetuated in the word *"nigger"* is manifested out of an arduous process of pain and inescapable *degradation and subjugation without deliverance* for the lmajority of Black People. Since its birth, the word *"nigger"* has withstood every test of endurance and attempted annihilation, only to continue to live and resonate in the hearts and minds of those whom relish it's sorted and twisted existence with little concern for its terribly painful and misguided past.

Word "nigger" ... Survives all wars and rebellions!!!

Who would have imagined that the use of the word *"nigger"* would have survived the Trans-Atlantic Slave Trade, British Colonialism, Indian Wars, Shay's Rebellion, Whiskey Rebellion, Fries' Rebellion, Barbary Wars, War of 1812, Mexican-American War, U.S. Slave Rebellions, Bleeding Kansas, Brown's Raid on Harper's Ferry, American slavery, American Civil War, Emancipation, American Reconstruction, Spanish-American War, U.S.-Philippine War, Boxer Rebellion, World War I, Great Depression, World War II, the Cold War, Korean War, Vietnam War, Iranian Hostage Crisis, U.S. Libya

Conflict, U.S. Invasion of Grenada, U.S. Invasion of Panama, Persian Gulf War *("Operation Desert Storm")*, World Trade Center and Pentagon attacks by Osama bin Laden & Al Qaeda, Afghanistan War *("Operation Enduring Freedom")* and Persian Gulf War *("Operation Iraqi Freedom")* among other minor military conflicts, wherein Black People sacrificed, struggled, fought and died for America's continued independence.

Word "nigger"...Memorialized and buried, yet it lives!!!

One decade ago the NAACP took on the mission of burying the so-called *"n"-Word*, only to find that the word continues to thrive and survive on *"life support"*. Ironically, its lingering survival is supported by Blacks who complain of being offended by its use by the descendants of those whom conceived and fostered it.

In fact the *"n"-Word* was buried in seriousness by the NAACP, but its symbolism was received in jest by a number of Black People. For if it had been a human corpse the burial would have been ruled an act of *"attempted murder"* and treated as a capital crime, simply because the word *"nigger"* was buried alive.

The word *"nigger"* has been condemned to *"death by lethal rejection"* in the public arena, due to the social pressures applied to the descendants of those whom fostered the word in the first place. Yet, the robust life that is continually witnessed is being breathed back into it by Black People who have become *"socially conditioned enigmatic human respirators"*. Sadly enough, far too many 21st century Black Folk are guilty of enabling its continued existence and use for reasons that defy human logic and rational comprehension.

Based upon the ceremony and pomp surrounding its burial and the nationwide news coverage that was provided by CBS, CNN, NBC, BBC, Washington Post, Associated Press, The New York Times, USA Today and The Detroit News among others, one would have thought the *"n"-Word* was in fact dead and permanently buried, only for it to continue to rear its ugly head and profanely speak on an ongoing basis.

I believe Reverend Otis Moss III, the Assistant Pastor of Trinity United Church of Christ located in Chicago, Illinois said it best when eulogizing the *"n"-Word* on July 9, 2007 upon stating the following concerning the word *"nigger"*...

"<u>This was the greatest child that racism ever birthed</u>..."

"The "n"-Word Gone Forever"

...or is it???

The new teachers of cultural dis-enlightenment!!!

This work has been written for everyone that is familiar with the 14th letter of the English alphabet, realizing that not everyone that read it will receive the message and agree.

The *"unsavory truth"* is that any unwelcomed pattern of social behavior will not be completely extinguished until the teachers of such behavior die out. When the *"enlightened ones"* among us abandon its use, in due time the *"socially unacceptable use"* of the word *"nigger"* will eventually go away, thereby sanctioning its *"official death"* and *"proper burial"*.

The *"teachers"* in this particular case includes both Whites and Blacks alike, who profane the letter *"n"* by continuing to use the word *"nigger"* and its *"derivatives"*, which has been reintroduced into the American society and it's lexicon as the *"n"-Word*.

Cultural and social implications of the word nigger!!!

For one to understand and fully appreciate the importance of discontinuing the use of the word *"nigger"*, we have to revisit the use of the word in its initial historical context to fully comprehend its *"social significance"* in the minds of White People, relative to the *"cultural dilemma"* that it poses for millions of America's African slave descendants.

When it comes to understanding this problem and addressing it at its root, I believe Malcolm X said it best in his speech, "<u>Message to the Grassroots</u>" that he gave at the Northern Negro Grass Roots Leadership Conference on November 10, 1963 *(Available, <u>Youtube</u>)*. The conference was held at the King Solomon Baptist Church in <u>Detroit</u>, <u>Michigan</u> just fourteen weeks prior to Malcolm's brutal assassination, which occurred following his split from the Nation of Islam.

Malcolm had this to say regarding the study of history...

"Of all our studies, history is best qualified to reward our research".

The study of West African history and its role in the Trans-Atlantic Slave Trade *(relative to the study of African American history)* is the key to understanding the fundamental problems of Black People in America, whom were forced into slavery to be used as the *"ECONOMIC ENGINE"* for constructing the *"New World"*.

When African Americans dig deep enough into the history of West Africa as it pertains to the history of British colonial slavery in America, we will find *"nigger" and "property"* buried at the root of our <u>social, political, economic, and family problems</u>.

- <u>Social</u> – Integration opened the door to social access for Blacks leading to the development of *"prejudice premium zones"* commonly known as *"suburbia"*. HUD *(Department of Housing and Urban Development)* was established in the aftermath of the Civil Rights Movement for the purpose of overseeing and managing the deployment of Blacks into previously owned and occupied White communities. PUD *(Planned Urban Development)* and recently enacted *"Stand Your Ground Laws"* are designed to work in unison for the purpose of redeploying Whites back into the urban centers that were abandoned by their predecessors beginning in the 1960s, when *"white flight"* took the form of a diaspora with inner city Whites flooding into the suburbs to escape and buffer themselves from the presence of Black People.
- <u>Political</u> – The birth of the Electoral College grew out of the pro-slavery movement as a means of buffering the vote in plantation districts and low White population areas with large concentrations of slaves *(without citizenship)* that were counted as 3/5 of a person in voter representation.

  The Electoral College came about as a result of the *"Three-Fifths Compromise" (Article 1, Section*

2, Paragraph 3 - US Constitution). The disparity was rectified by mandating 2 senators per state regardless of the state's population, leading to the disparity between the electoral votes outweighing the popular vote, which always leans conservative in national / presidential elections *(Al Gore vs. George W. Bush in the year 2000 and Hilary Clinton vs. Donald Trump in the year 2016).*

Voting rights and gerrymandering in addition to criminalization of the Black Race are measures that are designed to reduce the voting role of Blacks by miscellaneous means and felony convictions that are designed to favor whites as lessor offenders over Blacks.

- Economic – Unfair hiring practices, wage disparity, basic imbalance of economic empowerment, and historic job discrimination favoring Whites over Blacks.
- Family – The *"Willie Lynch Letter : The Making of a Slave"* is "THE BLUEPRINT" that was deployed during slavery for future containment, division, status reduction, and the ongoing plan to eliminate the Black male from the Black family equation. This racist agenda was further compounded by the welfare system guidelines of banning non-related Black males from household receiving aid, promoting the one parent Black family structure that is rapidly becoming the *"new Black family model"* of today.

Most importantly we need to understand that all of the anti-social measures and means that are used to target Black males, especially the younger Black males are systematically done for the purpose of *"population and voter control"*. The predatory police killings, high levels of incarceration, and role reversal between the male and female in the Black family are in the the *"<u>Willie Lynch Letter</u>"*. These measures were designed to quarantine the fertile Black and White females from the Black males' sperm.

All of these measures work in unison as *"birth control measures"* by isolating and destroying Black sperm donors for the purpose of suppressing child birth in favor of the Whites. *{<u>Read - Willie Lynch Letter</u>}*

The word nigger revisited at its source!!!

The saga of Africa's modern day American descendants began as an unbelievable tale of nightmarish proportion that redefined the *treatment boundaries* and *subject identity* of captives whom were initially kidnapped and forced-purchased into slavery for the purpose of constructing the *"New World"*.

In times past, prior to the Trans-Atlantic Slave Trade, slavery was based solely upon the loss of one's freedom, wherein the enslaved individuals became the servant property of another. In fact, slavery is not new; slavery has existed in various nations and lands since the dawn of humanity and the advent of mankind. Slavery is defined as...

> a.*"the state of a person who is a chattel of another"*
> b.*"something (<u>such as a slave, piece of furniture, tool, etc.</u>) that a person owns other than land or buildings."*

*A*frican slavery and its people!!!

*A*frican slavery existed long before there was an America and did not have its beginning with the Trans-Atlantic Slave Trade. Slavery in the Americas sprang from the birth of European enslavement that was forced upon Africans that had its beginning in the year 1441 A.D. with the Portuguese, whom initiated the practice of forcefully capturing Africans and trading them to the Europeans. Slavery in the Americas was considerably different from earlier forms of slavery dating back to the ancient civilizations of the Samaritans, Egyptians, Byzantines, and the Ottomans, among others. The earliest official record of slavery can be traced back to 1760 B.C. in Samaria, wherein the following is recorded in the <u>Code of Hammurabi</u>: *{Example: Law #15}*

> "If anyone take a male or female slave of the court, or a male or female slave of a freedman, outside the city gates, he shall be put to death."

*T*hose who lost their freedom to slavery prior to the Trans-Atlantic Slave Trade were fortunate considering they were allowed to retain their *cultural identities*. Unlike British colonial slavery in America, wherein the slaves were stripped of their <u>generational, historical, social, religious, ethnic,</u> and <u>personal identities</u>, which in effect constitutes "<u>institutionally prescribed nigger-dom</u>"? <u>In fact, "terrorism" and "identity theft" are believed to be a recent phenomenon, but both had their beginnings with the "life-lock" of British colonial slavery!!!</u>

*F*or this cause, Black People have a vested interest in learning the true knowledge of their cultural past that existed long before British colonial slavery began.

It is vitally important for Black People to understand that our historic beginning did not start with the off-loading of African captives from the slave ships that brought our ancestors to the American shores. For many of us, we treat our inception into the American experience as if our African ancestors signed up and agreed to a seven day Trans-Atlantic Cruise to America, only for the *"mythical cruise liners"* to breakdown at the scheduled time of departure, wherein our forefathers thought it best to remain in America and voluntarily work forever for free.

Well the truth of the matter is our West African ancestors did not arrive here in glee, sipping martinis, and drinking cocktails. Of course many would choose to simply close their minds to the truth, while immersing themselves in self-induced amnesia.

Malcolm X... *"we didn't land on Plymouth Rock,*

Plymouth Rock landed on us".

In fact the Mayflower and its host fleet of seafaring vessels were the 17th, 18th, and 19th century trans-Atlantic European cruise liners for the European immigrants who passed thru Ellis Island to become colonial settlers and American citizens, <u>but not us</u>.

The "Middle Passage" and its "floating hell holes"!!!

The story of Africans forced migration into the Americas was far different for the African captives whom found themselves strapped down and stored like sardines in the stench filled cargo holes of the slave transport vessels that journeyed to and fro across the Atlantic Ocean for 246 years, bringing Africa's precious human cargo to the Americas without a return option.

Unfortunately for the tens of millions that did survive the journey the transport vessels were nothing more than floating time capsules and *"life-long retarding incubators"* for those that survived the narrow storage confines of the lower deck compartments of those dreaded seafaring vessels.

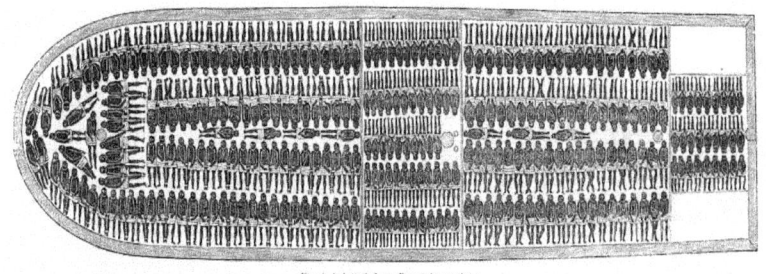

~ *Slave Ship Granger* ~

The original slave transport ships and the countless fleets of *"floating hell holes"* that traversed the treacherous Atlantic Ocean were death traps for countless millions of non-surviving African captives.

When we make the conscious choice of tracing our beginning back to the docking ramps of the various coastal shipping ports of colonial America and ending our search there, we not only do ourselves a grave disservice, but we also cripple those that come after us.

A once glorious people lost in cultural translation!!!

As a matter of future preparation, African Americans need to know that our native African forefathers came from a glorious past, prior to the European conquest of African enslavement. This knowledge would rid Blacks of the *"low ethnic esteem"* that negatively impacts us as a group. Esteem is the *"estimated outpouring"* originating from its root word *"teem"*, which means to *"pour out"*. It is impossible to estimate what and how much can be poured out of you, if you have no knowledge of what and how much has been poured into you by your ancestors.

When we allow ourselves and others to trace our

historical beginning back to the auction galleries and plantations and end our search there, we position ourselves to be defined as *"a non-distinct race of people lost in translation"*. The psychic tendency is to view ourselves as the *beggar* that got off the slave ship versus the *banker* that got on, or the *thief* that got off versus the *priest* that got on, or the *prostitute* that got off versus the *queen* that got on. We have been conditioned to accept the oppressors curse and disregard our blessing of heritage and prior greatness.

~ Charleston, SC Slave Market ~

The ancestral knowledge of Black People is essential to erasing the awful stigma that has been ascribed to us by our European slave masters of yesterday and only we can change the prevailing narrative and negative perception of ourselves. Our failure to reconnect with our history and greatness resigns us to the fate of a downtrodden people.

West Africans... Targets of European possession!!!

Our African and mulatto forefathers were labeled *"niggers"* in accordance with the commercial trade practices of the 16th through the 19th centuries that identified and labeled African captives based upon the regional areas from whence they were taken.

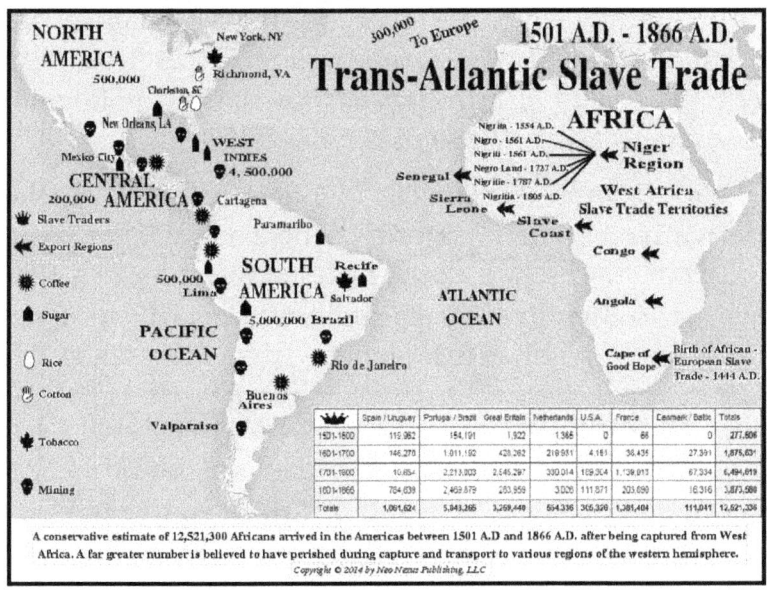

Cartography, which is the study and practice of mapmaking indicates that European maps from the late 19th and early 20th century were characterized by efforts on behalf of the colonial powers to identify the geographical areas from which their future possessions would be acquired.

```
                Gravé et Imp. par Erhard _ 2e tirage, 1888
┌─────────────────────────────────────────────────────────────┐
│          Possessions, Protectorats et Zônes d'action         │
│   Français        ▓▓▓▓   │  Espagnols        ░░░░            │
│   Anglais         ▓▓▓▓   │  Allemands        ▓▓▓▓            │
│   Portugais       ▓▓▓▓   │  Italiens         ▓▓▓▓            │
│   Turcs et tributaires ▓ │  Sultanat de Zanzibar ░░░         │
│   Les États marqués d'un grisé rouge ou laissés en blanc sont indépendants. │
│         Les Capitales des principaux États sont soulignées.   │
│   Les États réclamés par le Mahdi dans le Soudan sont entourés │
│                    d'un liseré à teinte neutre.              │
│      Z. Pays des Zoulous       N.R. Nouvelle République.     │
└─────────────────────────────────────────────────────────────┘
```

European maps of 19th and 20th century Africa identified areas abundant in raw material, mercantile goods and other targeted exports. European colonial maps of West Africa from the 16th through the mid-19th century were different, in that humans were identified as *"targets of possession"*. Slaves were *"the new commodity of extraction"* from the Niger Region, when the *"Trans-Atlantic Slave Trade"* began.

Early maps of Africa identify *"Niger"* as the derivative source from whence all of the *"EUROPEAN_GENERIC TRADE LABELS"* were derived that served to identify *"human captives"*, regardless of the areas and territories from whence they were taken.

> **An examination of the territorial labels that are inscribed on European colonial maps of West Africa, beginning in the 16th through the 19th century is the "critical key" to identifying the origin and misapplication of the word "nigger".**

Maps speak volumes about the present and the past. As early as 1554 A.D. foreign maps of Africa were being imprinted with the inscriptions *"Nigrita"*, *"Nigro"*, Nigriti, *"Negro Land"*, *"Nigritie"*, and

"Nigritia" identifying geographical defined areas of colonial slave acquisition within the Niger Region.

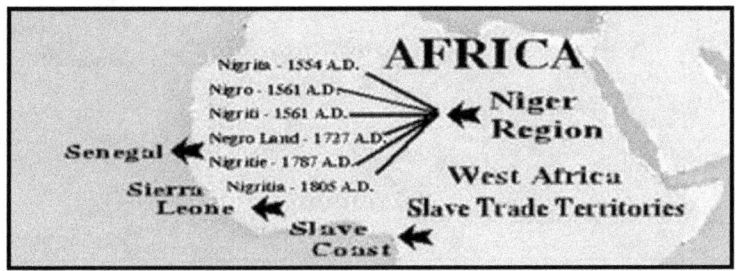

The territorial labels applied to the maps were inspired by their European colonizers. The natives were initially *kidnapped, stolen, and forced-purchased* before being traded and auctioned off in a loosely, coercive, mutual arrangement as *"niggers"*. <u>*In essence, the colonial maps represent the "X" that marks the spot!!!*</u>

Niger region... Targeted areas of slave acquisition!!!

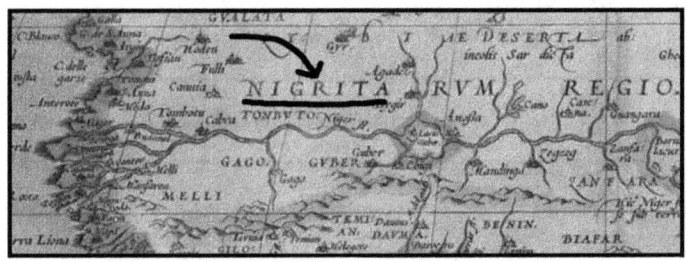

1554 (Nigrita)

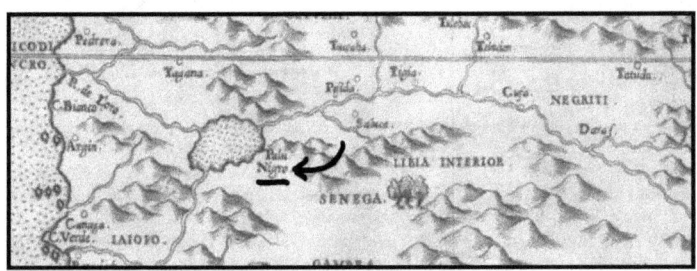

1561 (Nigro)

1575 (Nigriti)

1727 (Negro Land)

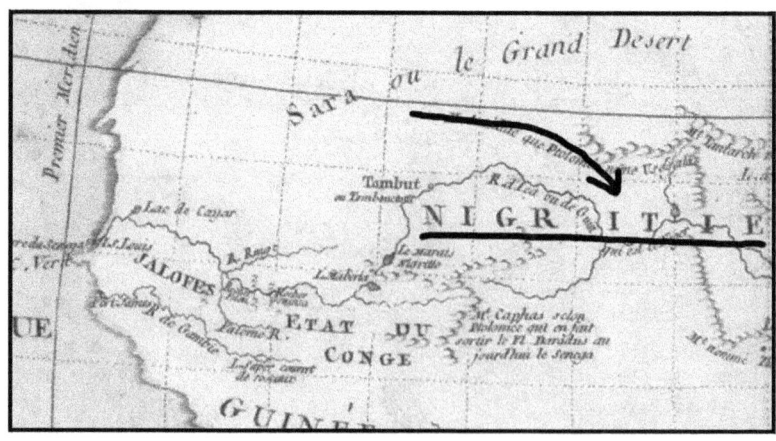

1787 (Nigritie)

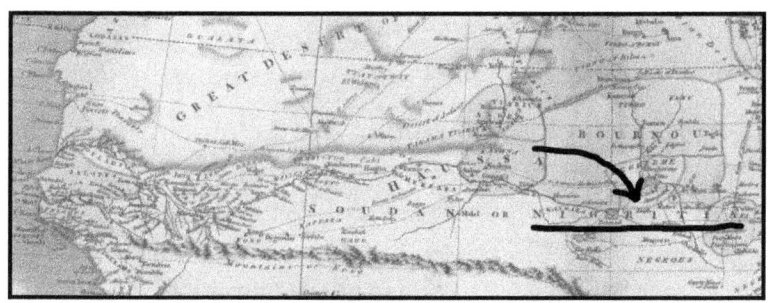

1805 (Nigritia)

How the word "nigger" came to be!!!

The word *"nigger"* evolved from the word *"Niger"*. *"Niger"* originated as a neutral term referring to people with black skin, a variation of the Spanish and Portuguese noun Negro, descendant from the Latin adjective niger *("black")*. In the 1520s Leo Africanus, a Moorish diplomat and author identified the *"region of Niger"* when referring to Africa's 3rd largest river as the *"river Niger"* located in the land of the Blacks.

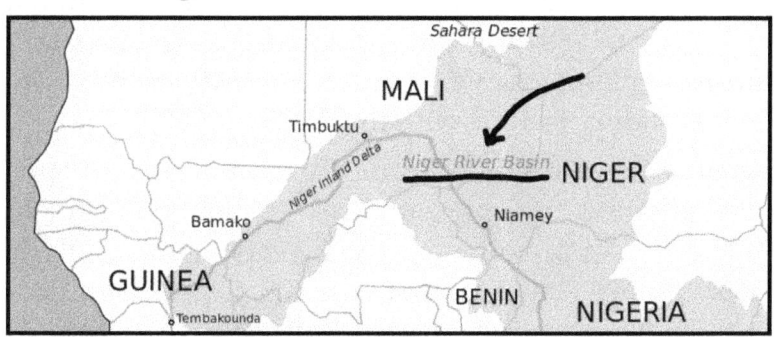

The word *"nigger"* is a *"descriptive thorn of rejection"* that was used to relegate the enslaved Africans to a *"last-class status"*. Prior to and after abolition it was common practice for Blacks to be referred to as *"nigger boy"* and *"nigger girl"* designating them as *"property"*. *"Nigger"* was rendered *"obsolete"* by abolition *causing it to be legally annulled on the basis of property,* wherein it was later substituted with *"Negro".*

Negro is a common noun that would inherit the English word usage of a *"proper noun",* making it a socially acceptable *"ethnic label"* under the law. Early Colonial maps of Africa were inscribed *"Negro Land",* but where is *"nigger land",* if not the *"Land of Dixie"*?

The word *"nigger"* did not begin as a *"racial slur",* although it did evolve into a *"derogatory badge of rejection"* due to slavery, later functioning to ridicule and exclude, in addition to relegating the African captives to centuries of inhumane bondage, coupled with *physical, psychological, verbal,* and *sexual abuses.*

Trans-Atlantic Slave Trade and its vestiges!!!

The Portuguese originated the Trans-Atlantic Slave Trade in 1444 with the capture of 235 Africans in 1441. The practice lasted 444 years before ending in Brazil on May 13, 1888 with the passage of the *"Golden Law".* British colonial slavery began in 1619, lasting 246 years, ending in 1865 with the American Civil War.

At the outset of the Reconstruction Period *"Negro"* was adopted to represent Black personhood, *but in title only.* Approximately three years later on July 9, 1868 the 14th Amendment to the U.S. Constitution was ratified granting citizenship *"to 'all persons born or naturalized in the United States,' which included former slaves recently freed."* The 14th Amendment elevated Negroes to the status of *"fully vested human beings",* no longer legally deemed *"three-fifths of a person".*

Though constitutionally free, Blacks were still

treated as *"second-class citizens"* under Jim Crow Laws, which were complimented with a constitutional loophole in the 13th Amendment allowing for its continuance for *"<u>convicted criminals</u>"*.

*<u>Section 1</u>. Neither slavery nor involuntary servitude, **except as a punishment for crime whereof the party shall have been duly convicted**, shall exist within the United States, or any place subject to their jurisdiction.*

<u>Section 2</u>. Congress shall have power to enforce this article by appropriate legislation.

This *"constitutionally sacred allowance"* paved the way for America's *"first prison bill"* that was passed by congress. Section one of the 13th Amendment left the door opened for a *"backdoor form of slavery"* that was immediately exploited to rebuild the southern economy and its infrastructure in the aftermath of the civil war. Shortly after its passage flagrant arrests were made from among the 4,000,000 unemployed previously freed black slaves, whom for the most part had no safe place to go and were consider *"vagrant de facto citizens"* needing to be arrested and put to work on behalf of the southern states and their constituents.

Criminalization of the Black race became the underlying theme of local and national politics, social policy, and race relations in American society leading up to the present, wherein 30% of the Black male population in Alabama have lost their right to vote.

The Bureau of Justice reported that 1 in 3 young Black males are expected to go to jail or prison in their lifetime. Black men account for 6.5% of the American population and make up 40.2% of the prison population. Upon being convicted of a felony offence,

Blacks are automatically reduced to *"3/5 of a person"* all over again, lacking fully vested citizenry rights.

*M*ass incarceration is the new form of Jim Crow that has morphed out of the evolutionary measures of racial containment born out Section 1 of the 13th Amendment to the U.S. Constitution. Jim Crow Laws were *"racial segregation laws"* enacted between 1870 and 1959 for the purpose of *economic restrictions, social containment, and political immobilization (*See Timeline – Ferris State University (FSU), Jim Crow Museum).*

I find it interesting that a current map of West Africa can be visited and upon viewing the coastal interior we will come upon two countries that are literally screaming out to us *"in name"*, revealing the source from whence the word *"nigger"* was derived. Those countries are... *Niger and Nigeria. Niger is a Latin word meaning "black"; pronounced Negro in Spanish and Portuguese. Nigeria is an extension of Niger, and <u>"nigger" is believed to be a mispronunciation of Niger by Southern Whites, when used as an "identifier of common origin" for our West African ancestors, whom were brought here as chattel property by their European traders.</u>*

*T*he following is quoted from the African American Registry, courtesy of Dr. David Pilgrim (FSU):

> *"In early modern French, niger became negre and, later, negress (Black woman) was unmistakably a part of language history.*
>
> *One can compare to negre the derogatory nigger and earlier English substitutes such as negar, neegar, neger, and niggor that developed into its lexico-semantic true version in English.*

It is probable that nigger is a phonetic spelling of the White Southern mispronunciation of Negro."

As a matter of fact, the word *"nigger"* was rendered obsolete in the aftermath of the American Civil War when the *Confederate Government, its currency and slave-based economy* ceased to exist; similar to the *"Confederate Flag"* that symbolized the *"INSTITUTION OF SLAVERY"* and the *"Confederate Money"* that it once generated.

THE *"CONFEDERATE 'WAR' FLAG"*,

"CONFEDERATE MONEY"

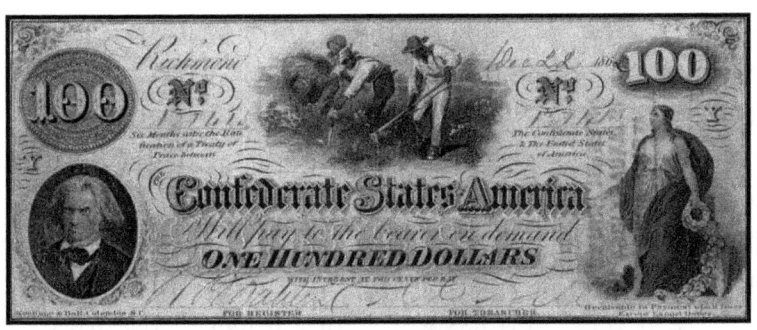

& *"NIGGER"* IS OBSOLETE!!!

Origin and evolution of the word "nigger"!!!

Upon researching the origin and evolution of the word *"nigger"*, it is not surprising to find that it has been relegated to the *"taboo column"* in American society in the form of the *"n"-Word*, which in itself is nothing more than a *"derogatorily ostracized pseudonym"*.

> **<u>Pseudonym</u>...** *"a name that a person or group assumes for a particular purpose, which can differ from his or her original or true name."*

A personal review of language history reveals an interesting fact, wherein only one word other than *"nigger or niggers"* which was derived from the true name of the slaves place of origin *"Niger or Nigers"* has undergone a phonetic transformation from acceptable word usage in the language of a people to a *"self-imposed pseudonym"*. This happened when the Hebrew word for *"GOD"* was relegated to the pseudonym *"YHWH" (pronounced "Yahweh" – "the 'Inexpressible Name' or 'Unutterable Name' of the God of Israel")*.

This was done by the Levitical Priesthood during the Old Testament era. In this particular instance, the word for *"GOD"*, namely *"Yahweh"* (*"The Most High"*), the Self-proclaimed *"I AM THAT I AM"* was expressed as the pseudonym *"YHWH"* for strictly pious and puritanical reasons.

Now the word *"nigger"*, unlike the word *"GOD"*, which represents the Highest of the High, represents the *"lowest of the low"*. Thus causing it to be exiled into the *"<u>bad word hall of fame</u>"* in North American society, where it has been assigned the *"n-word"* pseudonym for strictly socially pandemic reasons that serves as a euphemism to soften the impact of the word "nigger".

> **<u>Euphemism</u>...** *"the substitution of an agreeable or inoffensive expression for one that may offend or suggest something unpleasant."*

In review, it is plain to see how the word *"nigger"* having originated from *"Niger"*, conveys different images and meanings to different groups of people. Without knowledge of its origin, the sheer speaking of the word signifies different messages depending upon the *race, disposition, and social context* of the person or persons using it, be they White or Black. This denotes an evolution in the application of the word over an appreciable span of time during British colonial history and American history up until now.

Initially the word *"Niger"* functioned as a *"generic trade label"* that was affixed to all African captives brought into the North American British colonies, prior to being sold at auction and assigned *"proper names"*. Beginning in 1514 A.D. the African captives were being shipped from Sierra Leone and other coastal outposts into the various ports of entry in the New World. The *"generic trade label"* served as the captives' *"interim identifier"*, prior to them being placed on plantations wherein a *"first name"* was assigned by their owners that would become their property name.

The fact remains that the acquired subjects were traded and sold as *"captives without names"* to the

European merchants upon being taken from the European labelled West African areas of *Nigrita, Nigro, Nigriti, Negro Land, Nigritie,* and *Nigritia.* Between the points of acquisition and the points of sale the *British slave financiers, slave catchers, slave purchasers, slave transporters, slave merchants* referred to them as "NIGERS" in place of *Nigritas, Nigritis, Nigrities, Nigritias, Nigroes,* or *Negroes,* based upon the area in which they were taken. "NIGER" was used as an *"interim identifier"* to label the captives prior to the *"southern slave auctioneers"* and *"southern slave owners"* mispronunciation of *"NIGER",* which became *"nigger".*

Nigger...An "Interim Identifier" or "Racial Slur"?

Unfortunately, what began as an *"interim identifier"* for *"nameless captives"* based upon origin, prior to the captives becoming *"plantation slaves"* and receiving proper names, would ultimately become a permanent derogatory fixture of humiliation and verbal abuse.

In effect, the African captives were traded in bulk and sold without names by their African traders and European merchants. They remained *nameless* throughout the acquisition-to-auction process, at which time they were legally deemed slaves. They were later *dehumanized, prepped,* and *readied* for an extremely difficult and sometimes short, but extremely long utilitarian life on the *"plantation".* During the entire period of time they were being referred to as *"niggers"* by their handlers, while awaiting *"individual property names".*

Once on the plantations in the British colonies of America, the slaves received *"British property names" on a first name basis "only"*. A first name with no ties to family or cultural origin had the desired effect as do an *"inmate number"* that is assigned to convicts in the United States' Federal and State Penitentiary Systems today. *Inmate # "22843" was used to identify Malcolm X!*

Malcolm Little a/k/a Malcolm X was imprisoned from 1946 thru 1952. For 6 years Inmate Number "22843" identified Malcolm Little as Massachusetts' State Property.

El-Hajj Malik El-Shabazz {1925-1965}

Nigger... From private property to state property!!!

On and off of the plantations *"nigger"* was equivalent to *"convict"*, corresponding to *"PROPERTY"* and it carried the same social stigma and branding effect as it does today. The major difference is... unlike slaves on the plantations, the majority of today's prisoners are not confined forever and given good behavior they are allowed to go home. Slavery was different, there was no period of release and more importantly they had no home to return to. *The America continent was a "colonial Alcatraz" for the slaves!*

"Alcatraz Federal Penitentiary"

The North American continent, is virtually surrounded by water, making it very similar to the island of Alcatraz for the African slaves. Once on, it was virtually impossible to get off if you were a slave.

The surrounding waters served as a *"natural moat of captivity"* in both instances. America was the Confederate Alcatraz for Blacks before the Civil War!!!

Prison culture supplants early Hip Hop culture!!!

Unfortunately for African Americans, many young and middle aged male Blacks are *"emulating certain facets of prison behavior"*. By embracing *"sagging"* they are *"affirming the actions"* of those whom prefer that things return to the *"days of old"*. Sagging is a *"socially undesirable fashion of dress"* born out of prison culture.

Sagging is unmistakably a prison style of dress that congers up a mental image of Black People as "<u>post-dated niggers in the legal sense</u>", attired in shabby dress. Sagging is an "<u>undesirable fashion statement</u>" that creates images of Black People as *"property of White People"* in the minds of those who relish the idea of all Black People as *"slave property"*, belonging in "<u>institutions</u>". Prisons are extensions of the 16th through the 19th century plantations that were based on "<u>maximum containment</u>" and "<u>denial of citizenship</u>".

"Sagging" and its *"distasteful bedfellows"* serve as an open invitation to the wantonly guilty parties to reenact the *"racial ills of the past"* that are reemerging out of a brutal and dehumanizing, historical context. This in-part could account for the increasing number of Blacks being killed by White policeman, relative to the loss of *"public sentiment"* by White Americans. <u>**Sagging is equivalent to wearing *"red"* in a bullfight!!!**</u>

<u>*"Unfavorable Presentation"*</u>

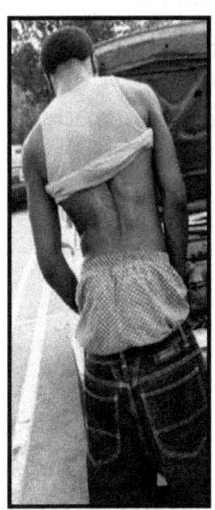  

<u>*"Generates "negative invitation!!!"*</u>

Loss of public sentiment... Key to social injustice!!!

"Public sentiment" is the fundamental key to *"justice"* and *"consensus"* in a free society. In the absence of public sentiment very little can be accomplished.

> *"Sentiment"* is defined as... *"an attitude, thought, or judgment, prompted by feelings of love, sympathy, kindness, etc."*

"Public sentiment" is a <u>social currency</u> that translates into "social acceptability" without prejudice or unfair penalty, when embraced by the general public.

"Public sentiment" is measured by the opinions and attitudes of the general public in matters of social and legal concerns, requiring "fairness in judgement" for the achievement of *peace, justice, and equality.*

Republican senatorial candidate Abraham Lincoln made the following statement, while debating incumbent democratic Senator Stephen A. Douglas during the 1858 Lincoln-Douglas Debates. A series of seven debates took place that is historically referred to as "The Great Debates of 1858".

"<u>In this and like communities, public sentiment is everything. With public sentiment, nothing can fail; without it, nothing can succeed.</u>"

"Public sentiment" was the deciding factor that lay at the very heart of the *"anti-slavery"* versus *"pro-slavery"* debates that propelled Attorney Abraham Lincoln to senatorial victory, leading up to his 1860 Presidential election. *Public sentiment* played a major role in the abolition of slavery and the American Civil War, including the 13th, 14th, and 15th Amendments to the Constitution, wherein Negroes received citizenship, civil rights, and voting rights.

Now, some 150 years later Black People in America find themselves caught up in a similar battle involving "<u>the loss of public sentiment</u>". The increasing numbers of Blacks being killed by *predatory White police officers* mirror the public lynchings that began during the Reconstruction Era, when *"public sentiment"* for Negroes was at its lowest at any time in America's post-slavery history.

<u>*Black Targets... Black People... Black Shootings...*</u>

<u>BLACK LIVES MATTER...</u>

"Casual Killing Act" once dead... Now resurrected!!!

Without doubt, the ongoing rash of police killings of Black people that is being witnessed is the reinstitution of the *"Casual Killing Act"* that was enacted in the State of Virginia in October 1669, when *"public sentiment"* was at its very worst. The *"Casual Killing Act"* of 1669 and the predatory police killings of 21st century Blacks have one thing in common... the notion of perceived failure of blacks to follow authoritative commands given by their white de facto owners. This rational provides justification to kill, when interpreted on the basis of *"Resisting the Master"*.

~ *Courtesy of Jim Morin @MorinToon* ~

On the basis of "PROPERTY OWNERSHIP", *"perceived disobedience"* by the police justifies the *"Right to Kill"*, just as it did during slavery when the plantation overseers and slave handlers were policing the slaves. This would suggest that even today all Black People are viewed as *"de facto property of White People"* in the minds of Whites and should be treated as "PROPERTY".

The *"Casual Killing Act"* received national exposure during the airing of *"Slavery and the Making of America"*, Thirteen/WNET New York on PBS.org...

"The Casual Killing Act"

Act of the Commonwealth of Virginia 1669 Cited in William Walter Henning. THE STATUTES AT LARGE; BEING A COLLECTION OF ALL THE LAWS OF VIRGINIA, FROM THE FIRST SESSION OF THE LEGISLATURE IN THE YEAR 1619. vols I and II. (New York: R & W & G Bartow, 1823)

DOCUMENT DESCRIPTION:

Overseers liberally applied violent punishments such as whippings to slaves they perceived to be transgressive. **This 1669 act declared that, should a slave be killed as a result of extreme punishment, the master should not face charges for the murder**.

TRANSCRIPT:

October 1669
Act I, 2:270
Charles II, King of England

An act about the casual killing of slaves.

WHEREAS the only law in force for the punishment of refractory servants (a) **resisting their master**, mistress or overseer cannot be inflicted upon negroes, nor the obstinacy of many of them by other than violent means to suppress, Be it enacted and declared by this grand assembly, **if any slave resist his master** (or other by his masters order correcting him) **and by the extremity of the correction should chance to die, that his death shall not be accounted felony, but the master** (or that other person appointed by the master to punish him) **be acquitted from molestation, since it cannot be presumed that prepended malice** (which alone makes murder a felony) **should induce any man to destroy his owner's estate**.

THE LACK OF "PUBLIC SENTIMENT" CAN BE...
A "LICENSE TO KILL" IN A RACIST CULTURE!!!

Self-castigation an enemy unto itself!!!

I believe the <u>apparent loss of public sentiment</u> among a large majority of American Whites in the 21st century is directly linked to *"self-castigation"* on behalf of younger Black folks who are totally clueless when it comes to the value of *"positive public perception"* in a multi-racial society. The social consequences apply to all African Americans who are struggling to overcome the *"last-class stigma"* that is associated with 246 years of slavery that ending just 150 years ago.

Importance of sticking to who we are as a people!!!

Berry Gordy, Jr. founded Motown Records in 1959 and within 5 years the *"Motown Charm School"* was established to promote a positive and professional Black image among his cadre of entertainers. *Mr. Gordy realized that <u>grooming, poise, and social graces</u> were needed by his artists for "<u>social acceptance</u>" in mainstream America. This was done at a time when <u>structural racism</u> was not constrained by law and camouflaged as it is today.* He understood the critical importance of *"positive public perception"* relative to *"Public Sentiment"*.

> *"Gordy told his artists that they were ambassadors for other African American artists who wanted to break into mainstream music and needed to act like royalty <u>to change the image that was commonly held by the white public at the time.</u>"*

> *"While not explicitly racist to have an in-house finishing school, <u>it does say a lot about what Berry Gordy at Motown wanted to present to the public.</u>"*

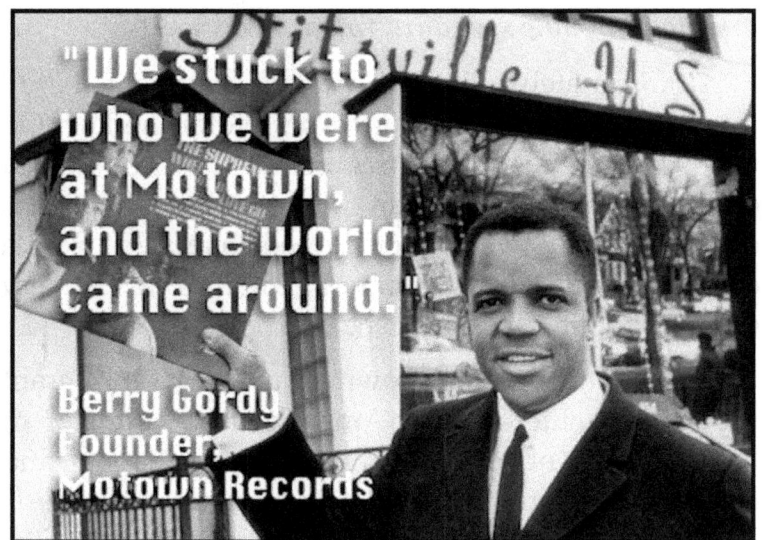

"We stuck to who we were at Motown, and the world came around."

Berry Gordy
Founder,
Motown Records

To fully understand the phenomenal importance and social impact of *"public sentiment"* upon Black's in America, Barry Gordy's statement should serve as a clarion call and constant reminder to all 21st century African Americans as it relates to our social conduct and personal behavior...

"We stuck to who we were at Motown and the world came around."

Sadly, the sacrifice and social discipline that was demonstrated by those who paved the way to the freedoms that African Americans enjoy today have been abandoned and ignored by the more recent generations of Black People, wherein the change of course has come at a grave and considerable cost.

This is especially true when it comes to the social assimilation of a minority group of people who were once slaves in a multi-racial society foundered upon racial discrimination against enslaved Africans and their descendants. *"We have abandoned who we were!!!"*

America's double standard toward Blacks!!!

Unfortunately, Blacks receive treatment based upon looks and behavior irrespective of the law. On the basis of historical treatment, we are viewed differently in the American family. Although citizens constitutionally, we are considered *"outsiders"* from a collective standpoint, based upon our slavery orientation into American society.

In fact, history as shown that every immigrant group that entered into America that were not of British descent received extremely harsh and discriminatory treatment. This is true for the *Polish, Italians, Germans, Jews, Asians, Hispanics, and the like.* The harsh and cruel treatment served as a form of initiation in exchange for American citizenship. The hostile and inhumane treatment was endured as a form of hazing for receiving citizenship into the American family. Once initiated, the hazing stops for every ethnic group except African Americans, whom were never intented to receive American citizenship due to slavery. *Black life in America is very similar to running a daily, medieval gauntlet of destruction, wherein millions are permanently damaged and totally destroyed!!!*

For African Americans, group acceptance is determined on a preselected basis that is deemed beneficial to the ruling class and does not equally apply to Blacks; *we are the social, economic, and political exception.* African Americans are yet to be fully integrated into the American family group, resulting in Blacks being judged by a different set of standards.

Consequently, the unfavorable actions and behaviors by those that have been fully accepted into the American family based upon their immigrant status are condoned and viewed as simple mistakes and alleged mental illnesses. Yet, when the identical actions and behaviors are committed by Blacks, we are socially condemned and branded criminals.

So we have to hold ourselves to a higher standard than other ethnic groups in American to avoid the *"negative social consequences"* that apply to us as *"outsiders"*, based upon our entry status into America as *"slaves"*. Unfortunately, history has shown that we cannot conduct ourselves like the immigrant masses that make up the ruling class in America and expect to receive equal justice and fair treatment under laws that were not designed to afford us equal protection.

Positive Image Presentation fuels Public Sentiment!!!

When it comes to *"personal presentation"* as it relates to *conduct, behavior, and dress,* we have to be at our best at all times. If not, *"negative presentation"* becomes a prescription for penalty and retribution for violating the *"social norms"* in American society. One would think that all Americans would be treated fairly and equal under the law, but when it comes to Blacks that is not the case, due to our slavery past. <u>We are ex-slaves!</u>

The legal treatment of Blacks is conditional based upon our personal presentation of self and public conduct as a people, relative to matters of *political, social, and economic issues* that are taking place at any given point in time. In essence, when it comes to citizenship we are treated like *"unwanted step children"*. Treatment of Blacks is based upon the ruling class' interpretation and appraisal of our civic and social conduct irrespective of the law.

<u>Younger Blacks must be told by older Blacks</u> that *"sagging"* although covered under the Constitution as a *"freedom of expression"*, is in fact *"indecent exposure"*. When one's underwear is being worn outside of one's trousers, partially exposing one's buttocks to the public, this is without doubt *"indecent exposure"* based upon any measure or standard public conduct.

Negative Image Presentation comes with a cost!!!

"Negative Image Presentation" breeds contempt in White society and causes pain and suffering in every sector of Black society, resulting from *"Black's... castigation of oneself"*.

"Castigation" is defined as... *"the act of being subjected to severe punishment, reproof or criticism"*. Castigation of oneself can cause an individual or group to be judged and penalized by a different set of standards than others in a given society.

"Self-castigation" can result from *"negative image presentation of oneself"*, which damages the *"public perception"* that functions to fuel *"public sentiment"*. Public sentiment has its advantages for a minority class of people, who are *"ex-slaves"* living in a society with a pro-slavery history and a racist past. Public sentiment can be the difference between the *"benefit of doubt"* being rendered by a Grand Jury with a *biased or racist prosecutor, versus being judged in the court of public opinion* where *"reasonable doubt"* is disregarded by a legal system and jury pools that favor exoneration of the guilty parties, while rendering unjust prosecutions upon the victims, <u>*especially when they are Black!!!*</u>

<u>*With public sentiment...*
casual killing could not exist!!!</u>

<u>*Without public sentiment...*
all injustices are possible!!!</u>

The *"lack of public sentiment"* makes everything legally admissible that fall *"outside of the boundaries of justice"*, including *racial profiling, excessive use of force, police brutality, false arrest, unjustified police homicide, illegal prosecutions and the like, that result in "guilty until proven innocent"* or *"socially condemned until pronounced dead"*.

Becoming a "Property Candidate" is a choice!!!

The unwelcomed *fashion statements, vulgar language,* and *public display of loose fitting behavior* congers up a mental image of Blacks as "<u>PROPERTY CANDIDATES</u>" alongside White People. Our public conduct congers up forgotten memories of our "<u>*slavery past*</u>" in the minds of those whom speak openly of "STATES SECESSION" and relish the idea of turning the clock back to a time wherein <u>"NIGGER" *was deemed legal on the basis of* "PERSONAL PROPERTY & PRIVATE OWNERSHIP"</u>.

Prior to the gears of the slave trade beginning to turn, there were millions of native Africans who never dreamed they would one day awake in a *"Gordon, the slave scenario"*. The indigenous west Africans were viewed as *"easy prey for capture"* based in-part on their scantily dressed appearance and native social habits. <u>*This should serve as a warning!!!*</u>

We desperately need to clean up our act!!!

The "FORBIDDEN TREASURE" of the 21st century free Blacks could be found buried in the hearts and minds of the 17th and 18th century African slaves and late 19th and 20th century Negroes' imagination. Dr. Martin Luther King, Jr. and Malcolm X among others fought and died to uncover that *"forbidden treasure"* and today it is referred to by all as the *"American Dream"*!!!

There is a thin line between *"poverty"* and *"prosperity"* that is quite similar to the thin line between *"dependence"* and *"independence"*. The thin line between *"poverty"* and *"prosperity"* is *"money"*. When all of the money is spent one becomes poor.

The thin line between *"dependence"* and *"independence"* is *"freedom"*. When the *"constitutional freedoms"* of a people are not used wisely, they become *"independence impoverished"* and are placed in a position of becoming the *"mistreated human property"* of those who are free.

Black freedom... A different kind of freedom!!!

Upon performing a careful review of Black history going back to the abolition of slavery it is clear based upon the emergence of Jim Crow Laws and the rise of the Klu Klux Klan that the freedom received by Negroes was a *"DIFFERENT KIND OF FREEDOM"* enjoyed by Whites. The freedom afforded to White and Asian citizens were interlaced with wide ranging liberties that were not afforded to Black American citizens.

In essence, there were *"two American freedoms"*, one for Whites who were truly free and another for Negroes and so-called colored people that came with restrictions, suppression, loss of life, mounting social restraints and economic oppression. The existence of the *"two American freedoms"* began in 1865 at the conclusion of the American Civil War and began to evolve under gradual change with the passage of the Civil Rights Act (1964) and Voting Rights Act (1965).

From 1965 through 2015, Black people have enjoyed 50 years of *"relatively unfettered American freedom"*, when compared to the *"Black Freedom"* of our past. For the past 2½ decades Blacks have been afforded the rare opportunity of constructing a path to "AFRICAN AMERICAN INDEPENDENCE". In hindsight, the first 25 years of freedom from 1965 through 1980 was built on the linear progression of those who came before us, only for a generational shift to occur that would change the focus and direction of our ongoing collective efforts and forward progress as a people.

A new generation in stark contrast to the old!!!

Beginning in the 1980's the actions and behavior of younger Blacks began to change, causing a major shift that would radically redefine the way in which Blacks are viewed in a social context. Up until this point, the earlier generations of Black People bowed their heads in humble acknowledgement of others versus nodding their heads. At the very same time, caps that were traditionally worn facing forward began to be worn facing backwards, signaling a shift in respect for tradition and authority. Interestingly, as nodding heads were going up, the trousers were coming down.

Trousers of Black youth that were traditionally worn waist-high began to sag across the buttocks, imitating prison culture. The embrace of *"thug life"* was ushered in on the backside of earlier, refreshing, and wholesome rap music, representing "*Rhythmic Articulated Poetry*". Only to descend into gutter-like vulgarity, wherein traditional rap music morphed into *"gangster rap"*, wherein *"nigger" and "bitch"* became the new taglines of twisted notoriety in music, cinema, and unfiltered public conversations.

In historical review, the last 25 of the past 50 years of *"relatively unfettered freedom"* has been spent dismantling the foundational pillars of *"public sentiment"* that provided the safeguards to a long history of continual progress without the constant threat of *"unchecked social reprisal"* by the policing arm of the establishment, while facing <u>*zero public outcry!!!*</u>

Freedom & public sentiment... Old social currencies!

"Freedom" and *"public sentiment"* are *"OLD SOCIAL CURRENCIES"* born out of the days of old that are used to *service* and *maintenance* "INDEPENDENCE". *"Freedom"* and *"public sentiment"* are the only social currencies that an individual or group has and only you can determine how it is spent…

<u>**BE CAREFUL HOW YOU SPEND IT!!!**</u>

Those who are poor in independence become the de facto property of another to do as they choose and this too is a form of *"SLAVERY"*, regardless of the name.

Far too many people interpret a positive change in social, political, and business behavior by old adversaries to mean that the hearts of the people have changed. In effect, what really changed were the laws.

<u>Congress has the authority to legislate laws,</u>

<u>*but in the absence of "public sentiment"*
it is impossible to... "legislate love."</u>

In fact, the very laws that were written to protect against *tyranny and evil* in a civilized society are used as shields by the *"wantonly evil doers"*. In effect, "THE LAW" is only as good as the people who are meant to enforce it. In the absence of *"public sentiment"* laws simply exist on paper, rather than in the hearts and conscience of those, who by virtue of their silence embrace the horrible injustices, which are known to exist and cause harm to others in a given society.

America's ongoing war with her own people!!!

> *"On Wednesday, after the announcement that NYPD Officer Daniel Pantaleo would not be indicted for killing Eric Garner, the NAACP's Legal Defense Fund Twitter posted a series of Tweets naming 76 men and women who were killed in police custody since the 1999 death of Amadou Diallo in New York." {gawker.com}*

On December 3, 2015 *"Huffington Post"* via *"Black Voices"* featured an in-depth report that was posted on *gawker.com* on December 8, 2014. The report detailed an extensive list of <u>*"unarmed people of color"*</u> killed by the police between 1999 and 2014. <u>The report chronicled a rash of Black killings by White police officers that began in 1999 correlating to a shift in the social behavior of younger Blacks, only to rapidly escalate with the 2008 election of Barack Hussien Obama being the first Black elected to the office of the American Presidency!!!</u>

Between the years of 1999 and 2007 14 unarmed deaths occurred totaling 1.75% per year, versus 62 unarmed deaths between the years of 2008 and 2014 totaling 10.3% unarmed deaths per year. The rate of unarmed deaths increased by 588.1% and continues to rise at an increasingly alarming rate leading into 2017.

> *Could the election of the first African American President Barack Hussein Obama have triggered the reemergence of an old phenomenon that was allowed to flourish unchecked due to the "loss of public sentiment" festering at its root???*

The following quotes were taken from the article... *"1 Black Man Is Killed Every 28 Hours by Police or Vigilantes: America Is Perpetually at War with Its Own People"*. The article was published on May 28, 2013 by Adam Hudson of AlterNet, based upon an aggregate study performed by the Malcolm X Grassroots Movement on the killings of Blacks:

> *"Police officers, security guards, or self-appointed vigilantes extrajudicially killed at least 313 African Americans in 2012 according to a recent study. This means a black person was killed by a security officer every 28 hours. The report notes that it's possible that the real number could be much higher."*

> *"Operation Ghetto Storm" explains why such killings occur so often. Current practices of institutional racism have roots in the enslavement of black Africans, whose labor was exploited to build the American capitalist economy, and the genocide of Native Americans.*

> *The report points out that in order to maintain the systems of racism, colonialism, and capitalist*

exploitation, the United States maintains a network of "repressive enforcement structures". These structures include the police, FBI, Homeland Security, CIA, Secret Service, prisons, and private security companies, along with mass surveillance and mass incarceration."

President Obama's election prompts secession calls!!!

In 2012, the Los Angeles Times reported that 50 states filed petitions on behalf of their citizens for *"secession"* from the United States of America desiring to form their own sovereign government.

> ## White House receives secession pleas from all 50 states
>
> November 14, 2012
> By Danielle Ryan
>
> "WASHINGTON -- What began as a small group of citizens voicing their disappointment with President Obama's victory in last week's presidential election has turned into a plea from hundreds of thousands of citizens to have their states be granted independence from the federal government."
>
> "The White House has now received secession petitions from all 50 states by citizens requesting that the administration *"peacefully grant"* them the opportunity to form their own sovereign government."

A petition drive culminated on November 14, 2012, expressing a desire on behalf of all 50 states to invoke the *"States-Rights Doctrine"* that provides argument for *"nullification of Federal Laws"* under the 10th Amendment of the Constitution. If successful, the Federal Government would have ceased to function as enforcement arm of the United States Constitution.

Without *"citizenry protection"* under Federal Law, things would revert to individual states being empowered to reinstate the *"Black Codes"* of the Jim Crow Era that restricted the freedom and advancement of African Americans prior to Civil Rights, reducing Blacks to "THE PEOPLE'S PROPERTY".

Property and nigger... Inextricably linked!!!

Historically speaking, the word *'"NIGGER"* when viewed on the basis of *"PROPERTY"* in combination with *"states secession"* and *"sovereign statehood"* creates a potential *"Jim Crow"* and *"Gordon, the slave scenario"*.

"Gordon, the slave: Harper's Weekly, July 4, 1863"

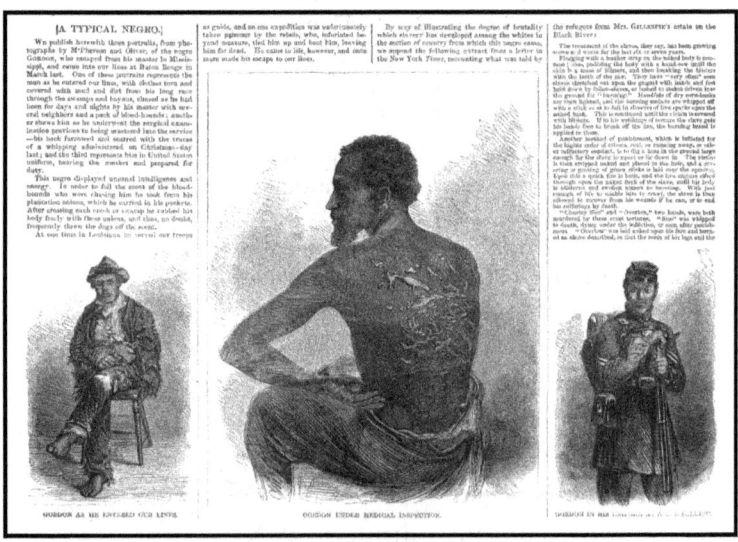

Therefore, the word *"nigger"* has negative value as a "<u>social currency</u>" when used in any context. It can only spend in the minds of those (*be they White or Black*), who relish the idea of Black People being in a "Master - servant" relationship to White People as their "<u>state property</u>" or "<u>personal property</u>".

*I*n 1705 the State of Virginia relegated <u>slaves</u>, <u>Native Americans</u> and <u>mulattos</u> to the status of property. So when White People refer to Black People as… "<u>NIGGER</u>" and "<u>NIGGERS</u>" they are in effect stating that the person or persons they are subjecting to this extremely derogatory and *"racially abusive branding"* are still the de facto *"legal property"* of White People. On a personal level they are asserting themselves as present day *"owner"* and *"Massa"*, issuing out of a foregone era.

*W*hen Black People affectionately or unaffectionately refer to themselves as… "<u>NIGGER</u>", "<u>NIGGA</u>", "<u>NIGGERS</u>", and "<u>NIGGAS</u>" colloquially, *we* are in effect *"openly inviting actions"* that are deemed utterly offensive. By communicating in this way, we are identifying ourselves with one another on the basis of "<u>PROPERTY</u>", which is clearly denoted by the use of… "<u>MY NIGGER</u>". This perpetuates a *"last-class image"* that equates all Black People to *"twenty first century slaves"* <u>unaware!!!</u>

The "mismanaged treasure" of the 21ˢᵗ century free Blacks could be found buried in the "chancery outcrop" of the African slaves' imagination, a treasure stemming from the "bedrock of racial inequality" that is known to all Americans as "Freedom"!!!

~ *Publisher's Note* ~

*On behalf of Neo-Nexus Publishing, LLC
I personally thank you for investing
your capital, time and energy
into the exploration of…*

"The "n"-Word Explained!"

"For The Socially Progressive"

*It is my sincere hope that
this long awaited publication
measured up to your expectations and
satisfied your literary taste as a reader.*

Charles E. Dickerson

~ *Cultural Acknowledgement* ~

"Munirah Uche Asha African Study Group"
~ "One Who Teaches Thought Life" ~
1980s thru 1990s – Columbia, SC
Sister Yvette Scott
Founder

∼∽∼

"Voice of United Africa"
1980s thru 1990s – Alexandria, VA
Brother Carl Kpoto
"Citizen of Ghana"
Founder

∼∽∼

www.ingramcontent.com/pod-product-compliance
Lightning Source LLC
Chambersburg PA
CBHW071319040426
42444CB00009B/2050